GW01338929

SHINE YOUR
MAGIC TORCH

Mysteries
of the
OCEAN

CONTENTS

THE ODYSSEY BEGINS
→ REEF AQUARIUM, AUSTRALIA ←
PAGE 6

RAINFOREST OF THE SEA
→ THE GREAT BARRIER REEF, AUSTRALIA ←
PAGE 8

FOREST OF GIANT KELP
→ THE TASMAN SEA, TASMANIA ←
PAGE 10

ANTARCTIC SEA ICE
→ THE SOUTHERN OCEAN ←
PAGE 12

MANGROVE FOREST
→ AO PHANG NGA, INDIAN OCEAN ←
PAGE 14

CORAL LAGOON
→ THE MALDIVES, INDIAN OCEAN ←
PAGE 16

UNDERSEA VOLCANO
→ WEST MATA VOLCANO, PACIFIC OCEAN ←
PAGE 18

ROCKY SEASHORE
→ SOLOMON ISLANDS, PACIFIC OCEAN ←
PAGE 20

DEEP OCEAN
→ MARIANA TRENCH, PACIFIC OCEAN ←
PAGE 22

ICY LAGOON
→ ALASKA, ARCTIC OCEAN ←
PAGE 24

THE WORLD'S AQUARIUM
→ GULF OF CALIFORNIA, PACIFIC OCEAN ←
PAGE 26

VENTS AND SEEPS
→ GALÁPAGOS ISLANDS, PACIFIC OCEAN ←
PAGE 28

OCEAN TEMPESTS
→ OPEN OCEAN, SOUTHERN OCEAN ←
PAGE 30

THE TWILIGHT ZONE
→ ATLANTIC OCEAN ←
PAGE 32

THE HIGH SEAS
→ ATLANTIC OCEAN ←
PAGE 34

COASTAL SEABED
→ OYSTER BAY, ATLANTIC OCEAN ←
PAGE 36

ARCTIC SEA ICE
→ GREENLAND, ARCTIC OCEAN ←
PAGE 38

The ODYSSEY BEGINS

Reef Aquarium, Australia

G'day and welcome to the Reef Aquarium! My name is William Jones and I'm a marine biologist, which means I study the oceans to learn more about these precious habitats. Here at the Aquarium, we show people the importance of protecting the world's seas, and we care for sick animals and plants too. Soon the creatures we are looking after will be strong enough to be returned to their coral reef home.

I'm showing my niece, Millie, the Aquarium before we set off on a great ocean adventure — an odyssey that will take us around the globe. I'm hoping to show her some incredible sights and uncover some of the seas' greatest secrets. As we journey, we will check the state of the oceans as the whole world depends on them staying healthy. I'm looking forward to getting out there!

Hello, I'm Millie and I'm so excited that Uncle William is taking me on this trip around the world. I know there are five oceans and they all connect to make one world ocean. But what lies beneath? How do animals survive in the DEEPEST, DARKEST WATERS?

Thankfully, I've got a special bit of kit with me – it's a MAGIC TORCH. It has the amazing ability to illuminate secret worlds, revealing sights that are invisible to most people. I'm really hoping it will reveal some of the ocean's mysteries.

Can you see anything unusual in the aquarium? Shine your magic torch!

RAINFOREST OF THE SEA

The Great Barrier Reef, Australia

The Great Barrier Reef is full of life so it's an ideal place to start our epic ocean voyage... and did you know snorkelling is one of the best ways to watch wildlife without disturbing it? There are many thousands of different types, or species, of creatures living in a reef, but many of them prefer to stay out of sight. If you move slowly through the water you can enjoy the glorious colours, but keep your eyes peeled for any movements, there are plenty of covert creatures nestled in between the rocky coral...

→ **WHO LIVES HERE?** At 2,300 kilometres long, this is the world's largest coral reef ecosystem and it's home to millions of animals — including the tiny creatures that built it. These coral polyps are related to jellyfish, but they live inside little rocky cups instead of swimming. Other tiny creatures that decorate this coral reef include Christmas tree worms: colourful marine worms that pop out from their tube like ornaments on a Christmas tree. These worms are sedentary, meaning that once they find a place they like, they don't move much.

SEA MONSTER There are big animals on the reef too, and some lucky visitors get to swim alongside whale sharks. I'm taking measurements of this beast to help my colleagues back at the Aquarium work out how old it is. We think whale sharks could live for more than 120 years! They are the biggest fish alive — and can grow to more than 15 metres long. Despite its great size and 300 tiny teeth, a whale shark is harmless. It sucks in mouthfuls of water and filters out the tiny animals and plants — plankton — that float in the water, before gulping them down. The colourful peacock mantis shrimp, however, lurks in the reef's nooks and crannies, staying hidden until it is time to ambush a victim — and wallop it with a killer blow!

Mermaid of the sea Seeing dugongs in the wild is a unique experience. The dugong is said to have inspired ancient tales of mermaids and, like those mythical creatures, they sing to each other underwater, using chirps and whistles to communicate. Mothers keep their calves close by their sides as they graze on seagrasses, rooting for them with their bristly, sensitive snouts. Like other marine mammals, dugongs feed their calves with milk and come to the surface to breathe in air. It's a shame we can't find one today...

Dugong   Christmas tree worm   Pygmy seahorse

I pulled my magic torch out straight away and what a surprise I got — a CHRISTMAS TREE WORM revealed itself! We must be careful as these worms retreat back into their burrows when startled. I slowly backed away, and as I did my torch's beam found a tiny, well-camouflaged PYGMY SEAHORSE.

I shone my torch over the seagrass and couldn't believe what I saw: a MERMAID OF THE SEA! Apparently, there are 600 different types of coral, more than 1,600 species of fish and 30 species of whales and dolphins in the Great Barrier Reef ecosystem — but there's just one type of dugong in the whole world.

Can you see...
◢ A dugong?
◢ A Christmas tree worm?
◢ A pygmy seahorse?
Shine your magic torch!

FOREST OF GIANT KELP

The Tasman Sea, Tasmania

A strange marine giant grows wild in this part of the Tasman Sea, which is cooled by currents of clear, icy water from the Antarctic. That makes it the perfect place for a type of seaweed, called giant kelp, to thrive. To explore the giant kelp forest Millie and I need our wetsuits and SCUBA equipment — that is Self-Contained Underwater Breathing Apparatus — our tanks hold a mixture of gases that we breathe through a mask. We can dive for just thirty minutes before it's time to return safely to the surface.

→ **GIANT KELP - A SUPER SEAWEED** Kelp grows fast, with towers of fronds that can reach up to 60 metres tall, adding 30-60 centimetres of height every day. The kelp forest creates a habitat for marine animals to shelter, breed and find food. Unfortunately, long-spined sea urchins are eating the kelp and destroying the forest. Millie and I need to find the sea urchins and count how many there are in this area so we can report this data back to the Aquarium.

THE LEAFY SEADRAGON
Seadragons belong to a group of slow-moving fish called seahorses, but the weedy seadragon looks more like seaweed than either a fish or a dragon! It can be hard to spot because it hovers next to the kelp and blends in perfectly with the surroundings. Seadragons, like other seahorses, suck food into through their long snouts and, unusually, it's the males that look after the eggs until they are ready to hatch.

Sharks that swell As we dived, I spied a swellshark cruising near the seabed, and pointed it out to Millie. Our movements scared the shark, which suddenly grew to twice its normal size. Ingesting water to make themselves bigger is a clever trick that swellsharks use to scare predators away. If they swell while hiding in a crevice they get completely wedged in for hours at a time.

Rock lobster   Red handfish   Old wife fish

I'm glad I had time to practise scuba-diving before Uncle William took me here — it was so cold I had to really focus on the job of counting sea urchins. I tried using my torch to help me count when I got a big surprise... I saw a ROCK LOBSTER instead. It grabbed one of the urchins in its claws and crunched it into bite-sized chunks. Those prickly spines didn't worry it one bit!

After that, I wasn't sure I wanted to shine my torch again but I'm so glad I did as it revealed a shoal of OLD WIFE FISH — they're difficult to see because their stripes help them hide in the kelp's shadows. Then my fingers froze and I dropped my torch. It fell onto the seabed and the torch-beam brightly shone on a RED HANDFISH. They are very rare, so that was a great treat, too!

Can you see...
◣ A rock lobster?
◣ A red handfish?
◣ An old wife fish?
Shine your magic torch!

ANTARCTIC SEA ICE

The Southern Ocean

Millie and I have travelled even further south, to visit a colony of Arctic terns that have flown all the way from the Arctic Ocean. We are actually standing on the sea here – it is so cold around Antarctica that the ocean freezes over, even on long summer days like today, when the sun won't set until close to midnight. Millie and I should have plenty of time to check the birds' transmitters, which track the birds as they go on their long journeys, or migrations, across the oceans. As a marine biologist, I am keen to find out how far these birds have travelled, where they may have stopped to rest and how they find their way from the North Pole to the South Pole, and back again – it's still a mystery!

Birds of a feather...
Chasing schools of small fish, Arctic terns plunge into the water at high speed and then rest on the Antarctic sea ice. We know about their incredible journey from the Arctic Ocean by looking at data from the transmitters. I have discovered that these birds flew 300 kilometres a day for nearly four months. Millie and I now need to check the terns are healthy and that the tiny transmitters are still attached to their legs before the birds return north at the end of the summer.

... flock together
I know Millie will be thrilled to observe a colony of emperor penguins, huddling together. I think she'd like to join them to keep warm! These big birds gather on the ice to breed and are perfectly adapted for life here, with a layer of fat beneath a blanket of waterproof feathers. Soon the grey, fluffy chicks will grow their distinctive black and white plumage. Then they will be able to swim out to sea, using their wings like flippers to fly through the waves as they hunt small fish, squid and shrimp-like animals called krill.

RICH PICKINGS The Southern Ocean is home to Weddell seals, too. They hunt Antarctic toothfish under the ice, and pop up from time to time to breathe, using holes in the ice. The water below is full of nutrients that help feed the plankton, which in turn become food for huge shoals of fish. I wish I could see the wildlife beneath the ice, but it's just too cold to dive in. I'd love to see an Antarctic octopus too. Like the toothfish, they have special chemicals in their blood to stop them freezing. These soft-bodied beasts use a deadly bite to deliver deadly venom that quickly kills their prey, but I'm keen to discover what tricks Antarctic octopuses use to keep their venom working at freezing temperatures. It's another marine mystery to solve!

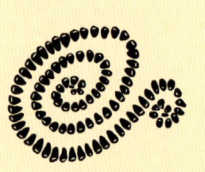

Salp

Antarctic toothfish

Antarctic octopus

Brrr! I'm glad we have enough warm clothes for Antarctica. I was helping Uncle William check the Arctic terns' transmitters when I spotted a seal's breathing hole. I shone my torch down and saw the slow movement of a small ANTARCTIC OCTOPUS. Then, all of a sudden, a huge, silvery ANTARCTIC TOOTHFISH swam past – it was nearly bigger than me!

Before we had to leave, I took a final look through the seal's breathing hole with my torch. A stunning spiral of blues and greens under the water took my breath away. I described it to Uncle William and he told me this was a SALP, a chain of small, soft-bodied animals that glow in the dark. How cool!

Can you find...
◣ A salp?
◣ An Antarctic toothfish?
◣ An Antarctic octopus?
Shine your magic torch!

MANGROVE FOREST

Ao Phang Nga, Indian Ocean

The next stop on our journey was much warmer — the mangrove forest, an important ecosystem found on the shorelines of tropical oceans where we are searching for a rare terrapin. A great way to explore mangrove forests is in a canoe or kayak. Paddling silently through the swampy water means you can observe the wildlife without disturbing the animals or damaging the trees.

→ **TURTLE MYSTERY** Millie's going ahead in her kayak to try and spot Chinese pond herons fishing with their long beaks and while Millie is busy, I'm going to watch the water's edge for signs of a northern river terrapin. There have been mysterious reports that one of these little turtles has been seen here in Phang Nga, but I think it's unlikely. Northern river terrapins are very rare and no one has managed to get a photograph of one in Thailand for years, so they are probably extinct here.

TROPICAL TREASURE A mangrove forest is a treasure chest at the edge of the ocean, with lots of exciting secrets to discover. The trees grow in slow-flowing water, their tall roots creating a dense network of dark hiding places for all sorts of animals. Prickly porcupine fish, for example, lurk in the shadows and only come out at night to hunt. They defend themselves from attack by swallowing air so their bodies swell and their sharp spines stand up, making them difficult to eat. Their flesh is toxic, too, so anything that tries to take a bite will soon regret it!

Ambush! Deadly hunters hide in mangrove forests. Crocodiles bask in dry, sunny spots, or lie motionless underwater, waiting for fish and crabs to swim past before pouncing with a quick snap of their mighty jaws. Even some fish, such as mangrove jacks, have a reputation as silent assassins that hide in the dark, waiting to ambush their prey. A sudden flick with a powerful tail stuns its victim and a single, snapping bite finishes it off.

Mangrove jack

Black-blotched porcupine fish

Northern river terrapin

Poor Uncle William was desperate to find a NORTHERN RIVER TERRAPIN, so I shone my magic torch on a tree root and there it was, basking in the midday heat! But as soon as the terrapin saw me, it dived into the water and disappeared, startling a BLACK-BOTCHED PORCUPINE FISH lurking in the shadows, which puffed itself up like a small, prickly ball!

Spotting a baby crocodile sunbathing was a real surprise, as Uncle William had told me they are rare in this swamp. As it was time to leave, I shone my torch for a final time, just as a MANGROVE JACK swam past the canoe and I caught a brief glimpse of its glistening scales.

Can you find...
◂ A mangrove jack?
◂ A black-blotched porcupine fish?
◂ A northern river terrapin?
Shine your magic torch!

CORAL LAGOON

The Maldives, Indian Ocean

Next we sailed west to reach the beautiful coral islands known as the Maldives, where I have a few surprises in store for Millie. It was evening when we first stepped onto the powder-white sand of the beach and, as the waves lapped the shore, a blue glow with sparkling white lights rippled across the water. This strange phenomenon is caused by plankton – tiny creatures that make their own light. Millie was thrilled by the sight, and even more excited when I said we can snorkel in the lagoon as the sun sets over the horizon, and search for an old friend of mine.

→ **MYSTERIOUS DEVILFISH** I wonder if the glowing blooms of plankton will attract some 'devilfish' to this lagoon? Long ago, sailors told tall tales of giant devilfish in the Indian Ocean that sank boats and drowned unsuspecting swimmers. The huge fish they had witnessed were actually harmless manta rays, but it's no surprise that sailors were fearful of these beasts because manta rays can grow more than 6 metres wide and look like scary, swimming bats. Thankfully manta rays, like whale sharks, only eat plankton and other small sea creatures.

A NURSERY FOR SEA TURTLES...
Snorkelling through the calm waters of the lagoon, we spotted my 'friend' - a large green sea turtle I've named Myrtle, swimming slowly towards the shore. This is the exact beach where she hatched from an egg – perhaps more than thirty years ago. Three years ago, I watched her lay her first clutch of eggs on this very beach and I now come back every year to watch her lay her next batch. Ocean scientists are now fairly certain how turtles find their way back to the exact beaches where they hatched: they can detect the Earth's magnetic field and use it as a map. I watched from a safe distance as Myrtle dug her nest in the soft sand. In about seven weeks, tiny turtle hatchlings will dig their way out of the sand and scuttle down to the sea.

... and baby sharks Coral lagoons are not just popular with sea turtles — reef sharks also love them because their young, or pups, are safe here from the bigger sharks that live in the open ocean. The pups and their parents hunt colourful parrotfish and shoals of bluestripe snappers that live in the lagoon. Parrotfish nibble at coral, crunching it up to reach the soft, tasty polyps inside. They pass out tiny pieces of rocky coral, which they can't digest, and much of the white sand on the beach here is actually parrotfish poo washed up from the floor of the lagoon!

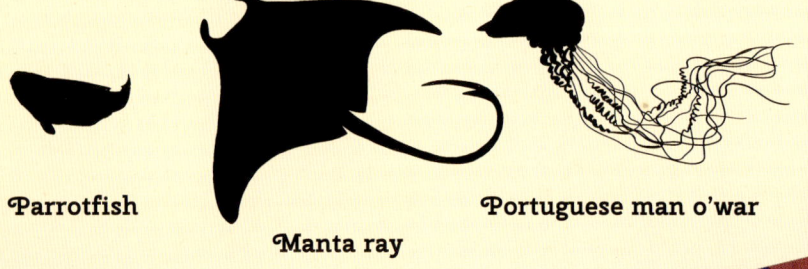

Parrotfish

Manta ray

Portuguese man o'war

My magic torch was perfect for revealing PARROTFISH. I was watching them eat the coral when Uncle William warned me to be on the lookout. He says a PORTUGUESE MAN O'WAR has been spotted in the lagoon, but its ghostly appearance means it is almost invisible in the water. Using my torch I've spied its long dangling tentacles — each one equipped with nasty stingers. We'll keep a safe distance from this phantom floater!

I was bedazzled by the sight of the twinkling plankton when I suddenly saw the dark, looming shape of something approaching. As I shone my torch, the magic beam revealed a huge MANTA RAY scooping up mouthfuls of plankton!

Can you find...
◣ A parrotfish?
◣ A manta ray?
◣ A Portuguese man o' war?
Shine your magic torch!

UNDERSEA VOLCANO

West Mata Volcano, Pacific Ocean

As night fell at the coral lagoon, I received exciting news from the Aquarium – a huge volcano was erupting near the Tonga Trench. A team of geologists were about to send a remotely-operated vehicle, or ROV, down to investigate the eruption – and Millie and I were invited to join them. I am particularly keen to find out if any deep-sea creatures can survive the heat created by an active undersea volcano so, after a long journey from the Maldives, we finally reached the team. They have sent the ROV into the depths, where it is equipped with lights and cameras. While this robot explores the volcano we can stay safe in the boat above, watching the action on a screen.

→ **FIRE AND FUMES** An astonishing sight greeted us! We have been watching lava pouring out of the volcano's central vent in red and gold streams. Metre-wide bubbles of lava also rise upwards, alongside billowing clouds of milky-yellow gases. Occasionally, a sudden blast sends lumps of hot rock flying all around – just missing the ROV! I doubted anything could survive here, but there are some fascinating signs of life including rattail fish, which are common in deep waters. I wonder if we might see Pompeii worms - I know they can survive in water at a blistering 300 degrees Celsius but I have never heard of them surviving this close to lava flows.

STRANGE SURVIVORS
Scientists have discovered all sorts of strange creatures around undersea mountains including squat lobsters, but there has been little research into life around active volcanoes. Perhaps the ROV will pick up signs of barreleye fish – I have never seen them in waters this deep before. These bizarre creatures can see through the top of their transparent heads. They have tube-shaped eyes that they rotate so they can look up and spot anything swimming above them.

Scavengers What luck! The ROV's light beams illuminated the body of a whale on the seabed, a short distance from the volcano. The whale had probably died of natural causes and sank to the bottom of the ocean, where a horde of scavengers is feasting on its remains. A giant isopod caught my eye – it looks like a large woodlouse. Even swarms of amphipods – small shrimp-like animals - are having a meal. The great heat does not seem to have disturbed these tough little scavengers, so I shall report this exciting discovery back to the Aquarium.

Pompeii worm    Squat lobster    Barreleye fish

I didn't expect it but my magic torch worked on the screen! I used it to reveal some mysterious animals that were hidden from the ROV's powerful beams of light. Near the volcano, a POMPEII WORM poked its bristly body out of its burrow and a curious SQUAT LOBSTER swam over to investigate. Uncle William said it was probably hoping for a worm-sized snack...

The highlight of this trip was seeing a BARRELEYE FISH. Having a see-through head must be very strange, but I guess if you are a fish it's handy to know what's happening in the water above you... so you can make a quick escape if you need to!

Can you find...
◢ A Pompeii worm?
◢ A squat lobster?
◢ A barreleye fish?
Shine your magic torch!

ROCKY SEASHORE

Solomon Islands, Pacific Ocean

After all the excitement of watching the volcano erupt, Millie and I thought we might enjoy a bit of a relaxation by the rock pool. This is a marvellous place to watch ocean wildlife, but it will also give me the chance to search for some of the world's deadliest ocean creatures. At the Aquarium, we have been doing some research into their venom so we can develop medicines, or antivenoms, that will help people who have been stung or bitten. One day, some of these venoms could be adapted to treat diseases too — like, did you know snake venoms are already used to treat heart disease?

→ **EBB AND FLOW** As the water ebbs (moves away from the land), it reveals some mysterious creatures, stranded in rock pools for just a few hours. When the tide comes in and water flows over the shore once more, the rock pools will disappear. We only have a short time to explore here, and Millie and I will need to take extra care. We are on the hunt for some animals with deadly venom, and many of them have colours and patterns that help to camouflage them against seaweed, coral and rocks.

Toxic terrors Venom is a poison that is injected, usually by teeth, spines, stingers or claws. While some venomous animals - including lionfish and sea kraits - use colours, stripes or bold colours to warn others that they are dangerous, others prefer to hide instead. Stealthy stonefish are almost invisible on the seabed, but they are equipped with a sharp spine that delivers a deadly dose of venom to anyone who accidentally treads on it. Even sea cucumbers, which look harmless, can cover predators with sticky, poisonous threads that shoot out of their bottoms! Finding some of the venomous animals has been quite easy but, sadly, I failed to spot any sea cucumbers or stonefish...

DANCING BIRDS The rocky shore is a perfect habitat for many seabirds, including red-footed booby birds. The reason for their colourful feet was a mystery until people watched them dance! Like many birds, male boobies use their dancing skills to impress their mates, and red feet make sure that the females notice their fancy moves. While I was watching a booby dancing I noticed a smaller sea bird nearby, fishing in a rock pool. It was a Beck's petrel, which is so rare that it is at risk of extinction. Another discovery the Aquarium will be thrilled to learn about!

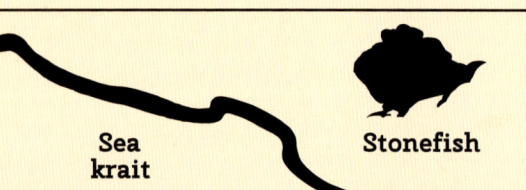

Sea krait | Stonefish | Sea cucumber

Uncle William insisted that I wear thick boots for wading in the rock pools to protect myself from venomous animals. I knew I'd be even safer if I could see them with my magic torch. As I shone the light into the rock pool I located a STONEFISH under the coral, and a PINEAPPLE SEA CUCUMBER crawling along the bottom. Apparently some people like to eat these soft, squishy animals, but I'm not tempted!

I was about to put my torch away, but decided to take one final peek into the rock pool. What a fright I got! A YELLOW-LIPPED SEA KRAIT was slithering out of the water, heading towards the shore. Uncle William says that although sea kraits have some of the world's deadliest venom, these snakes rarely bite. But I wasn't taking any chances...

Can you find...
◀ A sea krait?
◀ A stonefish?
◀ A sea cucumber?
Shine your magic torch!

DEEP OCEAN

Mariana Trench, Pacific Ocean

Millie and I had to abandon our plan to spend a few days enjoying the rocky seashore because I got an urgent call from the Aquarium. An expedition to the Mariana Trench - the deepest part of the World Ocean — was in trouble and needed our help; their marine biologist was unwell. Of course, I offered to go in their place. Travelling to the deep in a submersible has to be one of the most dangerous journeys any ocean explorer can take, but it is also the most thrilling. There are lifeforms never before seen by human eyes and we couldn't miss an opportunity like this.

→ **WHAT PRESSURE!** More people have been to the Moon than have travelled 11,000 metres to the very bottom of the Mariana Trench. We descended 3,000 metres in a submersible, where we can watch mysterious creatures of the deep through the windows. Down here the water is pitch-black, near freezing and its huge weight creates a bone-crushing pressure. Thankfully, the submersible has thick metal walls, a bank of strong lights and cameras so we can capture any signs of life. My job is to observe, film and make notes about any animals we see.

PUTTING ON A LIGHT SHOW
The deep sea may be dark, but many animals here are bioluminescent - which means they can make their own light! Some of them do this using special organs called photophores. A gulper eel has photophores in its tail to lure prey to come close then snaps them up in one gulp. Its mouth is so large it can eat fish or crabs bigger than itself. Tiny vampire squid are covered in photophores, which they probably flash to scare predators away. Like dumbo octopuses, these squid have ear-like fins that they use to flap their way through the water as they search for something to eat.

Fang-toothed monster We have been lucky to spot several animals already, but there is something else I am desperately looking for: a viperfish. Viperfish have huge fang-like teeth and a long spine on the back of the head. The spine is tipped with a photophore, which flashes brightly to tempt curious prey to come close. Few people have ever seen one of these monsters, and it's my dream to be the first person to film this predator attack its prey in the Mariana Trench.

Deep sea glass squid

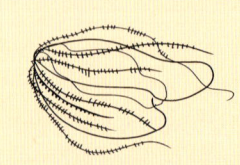

Viperfish

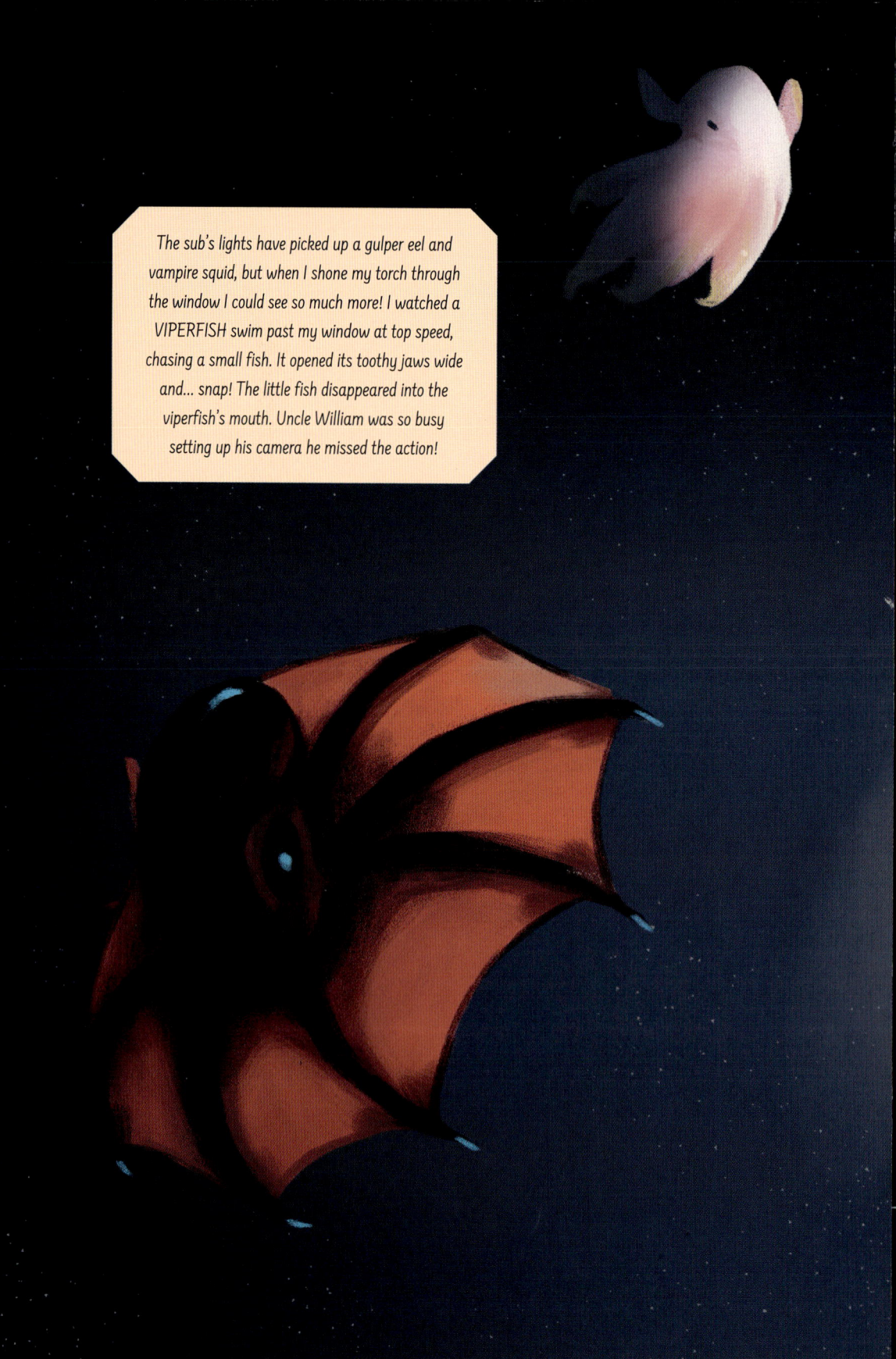

Comb jelly

The sub's lights have picked up a gulper eel and vampire squid, but when I shone my torch through the window I could see so much more! I watched a VIPERFISH swim past my window at top speed, chasing a small fish. It opened its toothy jaws wide and... snap! The little fish disappeared into the viperfish's mouth. Uncle William was so busy setting up his camera he missed the action!

My magic torch is especially good at revealing animals that are transparent, such as a DEEP SEA GLASS SQUID, which has enormous eyes. No one else on the submersible could see the squid, or a COMB JELLY, which shimmered with amazing colours. It was covered with rows of hair-like threads, called cilia. When the cilia beat, the jelly moves forward and glows. It was so beautiful, like fairy lights in the dark.

Can you find...
- A deep sea glass squid?
- A viperfish?
- A comb jelly?

Shine your magic torch!

ICY LAGOON

Alaska, Arctic Ocean

A long voyage across the Pacific has brought us to the next stage of our adventure in the Arctic Ocean. We are exploring a coastal lagoon, where the ocean is shallower and calmer than further out to sea, creating a haven for wildlife. Spring is coming here in the north, so the weather is warming up and the sea ice is beginning to melt. I'm investigating this important habitat to discover how the change of season attracts animals to the lagoon, where they find a safe place to mate and have their young. It's so exciting to see signs of new life all around us.

→ **SPRING BABIES** In spring, many migrating animals make their way to the lagoon, including beluga whales, which give birth here after May. Red-necked phalaropes also come to the lagoon to lay their eggs, after spending the winter out at sea. I've spotted several red-necked phalaropes preparing to nest here, but they have arrived sooner than expected — I think that's because the Arctic sea ice is melting earlier every year. Our guide, Arnaaluk, says that the way the world's weather is changing is having a big impact on the Arctic. She has already seen sockeye salmon in the lagoon, on their way upriver to lay their eggs... that's earlier than usual, so I will keep my eyes peeled for them.

Canaries and unicorns

Centuries ago, people reported hearing singing mermaids in the Arctic, and seeing marine unicorns swim in the icy seas. The mysterious beasts they had witnessed were not really mythical creatures, but two types of small whale — narwhals and white beluga whales. Narwhals are called unicorns of the sea because they have one bizarre, long tooth that looks like a unicorn's horn. This tusk can grow to 3 metres long and no one is sure why narwhals have tusks... another mystery to be solved one day! Beluga whales are called sea canaries because they talk to each other with cheerful chirps and whistles. I'm sure Millie will agree with me that belugas and narwhals are just as magical as mythical beasts.

PUPS AND CALVES

When you watch seals and walruses on land they look heavy and slow, but as soon as these smooth-skinned mammals slip into the water they can slip through the waves with grace. Arnaluuk has spotted some walruses with their calves on the rocky beach. If we are lucky we may also see a ringed seal on some sea ice — the seals prefer to stay away from the coast because polar bears live there, and they try to eat them!

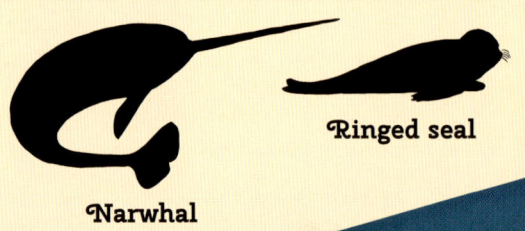

Sockeye salmon

Narwhal

Ringed seal

A milky-skinned beluga whale and her baby swam alongside our boat - what a beautiful sight. I wanted to see more, so I shone my torch down into the water and it revealed a NARWHAL nearby. It poked its horn out of the water, as if it was waving at me!

I pointed the beam of my torch deep into the inky water alongside the boat and saw a SOCKEYE SALMON, whipping its powerful tail from side to side as it swam towards the coast. As we passed an ice floe, I shone my torch on its surface and low and behold there was a RINGED SEAL, resting on the ice. I hope a polar bear doesn't see them!

Can you find...
- A sockeye salmon?
- A narwhal?
- A ringed seal?

Shine your magic torch!

THE WORLD'S AQUARIUM

Gulf of California, Pacific Ocean

We headed south to warmer waters, where I will investigate a strange phenomenon that has been reported in the Gulf of California. These turquoise waters are often called the world's aquarium as they are home to a huge number of fish and cetaceans – that's members of the whale, porpoise and dolphin family. However, in recent years the number of fish has been falling, while the number of squid has been growing. The local fishermen are worried by the mysterious disappearance of the fish, and have asked me to help.

Red devil invasion Humboldt squid are called red devils because they look scary when they are under attack from predators. They leap out of the water and turn crimson! Fifty years ago these squid were rarely seen in the Gulf but now they are common, while fish such as striped marlins and tuna are becoming rare. Some fishermen think the squid are the problem, but that's not true. Young squid are usually eaten by the marlins and tuna, but as too many of these big fish are taken from the ocean, it means more squid are surviving. This problem will get worse unless the fishing boats take fewer fish from the Gulf, and let their populations recover.

SECRET CETACEANS
We are exploring the Gulf using special rebreather scuba equipment. It is less noisy and makes fewer bubbles so it won't disturb the cetaceans. Grey whales come here to give birth to their calves, but it is another cetacean I really want to see: the vaquita. This is the only place in the world where this elusive, and extremely rare, porpoise lives. Sadly, vaquitas have almost gone extinct because they get caught in the fishing nets, so it's very unlikely we will see one.

→ **DEMON SHARK** There have been reports of a huge black shark living in the deep waters of the Gulf, but I have seen no sign of it. I think it's likely the local fishermen have seen the shadow of a whale and mistaken it for their 'demon shark'.

However, Millie and I have enjoyed watching scalloped hammerhead sharks chasing fish and squid. Their eyes are set on the sides of their hammer-shaped heads and this allows them to see prey more easily, and judge how far away it is more accurately.

Vaquita **Striped marlin** **Great white shark**

There are probably fewer than twenty VAQUITAS in the world, so you can imagine how excited I was when I saw one. It was chasing a young STRIPED MARLIN, which was swimming as fast as it could towards the open sea. Uncle William said marlins are not as rare as vaquitas, but if no one takes steps to protect them, they may become endangered, too.

I was terrified when I saw a dark shadow swimming below us so I shone my magic torch to investigate. The beam revealed that it was a GREAT WHITE SHARK. Uncle William explained that these sharks occasionally have such dark skin that they appear black. Thankfully, we hadn't seen a demon... but it's not wise to stay in the water with a great white shark either, so we swiftly returned to our boat!

Can you find...
◣ A vaquita?
◣ A striped marlin?
◣ A great white shark?
Shine your magic torch!

VENTS AND SEEPS

Galápagos Islands, Pacific Ocean

Millie was a little confused when I told her that our next stop would involve feather dusters, chimneys and black smoke... We are exploring another deep sea habitat, but this one has a collection of creatures that are adapted to survive in a lethal soup of poisonous chemicals. We are at a hydrothermal vent — a deep crack in the seabed. Seawater that seeps into the vent is heated to a phenomenal 400 degrees Celsius and dissolves minerals in the rock, turning them into a foul liquid that would kill most forms of life. The first time I came here I was amazed at the bizarre life forms I found... and I expect there will be more surprises in store this time, too!

→ **BLACK SMOKERS** Our deep sea submersible has brought us to a depth of about 2,000 metres but we are staying a safe distance from the superheated water. Black 'smoke', which is actually hot water mixed with the toxic chemicals, is belching out of tall chimneys. This habitat should be hostile to life, but we are spotting new species of animals all the time at hydrothermal vents. Being here is a great opportunity to spot an animal that no human has ever seen before. That's an exciting prospect for a biologist like me!

DEEP SEA SOUP A vent tube worm lacks a mouth but the red part of its body collects minerals from the superheated, soupy water. The minerals feed bacteria that live inside the worm's body, and the bacteria then make food for the worm. Feather duster worms, however, have unusual fluffy tentacles that are covered in bacteria. The bacteria feed on the gases that come out of the vent, and the worms then eat the bacteria. What ingenious ways to survive!

Yeti crabs Several types of ghostly crab have been spotted around hydrothermal vents before, but Millie and I have spotted a brand new type. This is a very exciting discovery! These creepy crustaceans are called yeti crabs because they look furry, but the 'hairs' on their pincers contain bacteria, which the crabs eat. Yeti crabs are all given the scientific name 'Kiwa', so this new species will be named Kiwa mortimeri, as we discovered it.

Vent fish

Giant sea anemone

Brittlestar

As Uncle William was taking photographs of the new yeti crab, I pulled out my magic torch and shone its bright beam around the hydrothermal vent. To my surprise, there was a small, slender VENT FISH swimming between the tube worms. It looked like it was heading towards a BRITTLESTAR. Brittlestars usually feed by scavenging food from the water, but larger ones can grab shrimp and squid.

I swung the torch round to the other window which revealed a GIANT SEA ANEMONE floating past. Most anemones are attached to the seabed, but this one could swim. It trailed its long pink tentacles behind as it moved towards the vent. How such a delicate-looking creature could survive this hot, toxic habitat is a mystery to me.

Can you find...
- A vent fish?
- A giant sea anemone?
- A brittlestar?

Shine your magic torch!

OCEAN TEMPESTS

Open Ocean, Southern Ocean

We must battle through high winds, strong currents and tall crashing waves to reach the calmer waters of the Atlantic Ocean. We are passing through the Southern Ocean to reach our next destination but this part of the journey is particularly dangerous. It is fiercely cold here, but there are animals that call this wild place home. I am not sure that we will be able to see many of them though — the rain is lashing the boat, making it almost impossible to see anything beyond the ends of our noses! I was hoping to catch sight of the elusive colossal squid — few people have ever seen this monster living in the ocean.

→ **A FIGHT FOR SURVIVAL** While we battle the weather above water, deadly fights are also taking placing in the cold waters below. Chinstrap penguins dive through the water, chasing shoals of krill, but they must keep a look out for predators at the same time. Leopard seals and orcas have speed, strength and power on their side — thankfully the luckiest penguins are able to leap out of the water to seek refuge on floating icebergs.

COLOSSAL SQUID Many years ago, a rare colossal squid was caught in these waters. It measured an astonishing 10 metres long, from the top of its head to the tip of its longest tentacles. How these animals live their lives is a total mystery as few people have seen one, and no one has ever been able to observe it underwater. A colossal squid's eyes can grow as big as dinner plates and its long tentacles are equipped with 25 hooks — perfect for grabbing large fish as they swim past.

Antarctic krill The cold waters of the Southern Ocean are rich in food for the massive swarms of shrimp-like krill that thrive here. The krill are then eaten by all sorts of other animals, including icefish and albatrosses. Although a single krill is no bigger than your finger, these little pink creatures are the main food for the giants of the ocean — blue whales — which swim here to feast. One blue whale can eat six tons of krill in a single day, and then produces floating clouds of pink poo!

Antarctic krill

Orca

Colossal squid

This has been the most amazing day of the whole trip so far! When we arrived here, I wondered how we could see anything in this wretched storm. But as I shone my magic torch's beam out to sea, I was delighted to see an ORCA leaping out of the water, and I actually think it enjoyed splashing in the rain!

Suddenly, I noticed dark shadows passing under the boat and so I shone my torch below. I made out long trailing tentacles before I realised I was looking at the unmistakable shape of a juvenile COLOSSAL SQUID on the hunt for ANTARCTIC KRILL! Result!

Can you find...
◣ Antarctic krill?
◣ An orca?
◣ A colossal squid?
Shine your magic torch!

THE TWILIGHT ZONE

Atlantic Ocean

We are now plunging deep below the waves for the final time, heading into the part of the ocean called the twilight zone. At a depth of over 200 metres below the surface, this spooky place has just enough sunlight for animals to be able to see. This part of the Atlantic has barely been explored, and the creatures of the twilight zone are mostly unknown, so this will be an exciting trip for me and Millie. We are in the sub, diving just as the day dawns, so we should see signs of one of the world's most incredible journeys, as animals move down from the sunlit waters to the safety of the deeper, darker water, where it's harder for predators to find them.

→ **A SECRET WORLD OF SHARKS** There are goblins and megamouths here in the twilight zone. The goblin shark has rarely been seen in the wild, so its lifestyle remains a mystery. It has a pink, flabby body and a long, strange snout, which may help it find prey by detecting the electricity made by other fish's muscles. Its strange jaws can shoot out of its mouth to grab its victim with dagger-like teeth. Megamouth sharks are bigger, but far less dangerous because they eat plankton. It would be amazing to spot a megamouth here — very few have ever been seen…

Flashing mirrors Fish of the twilight zone, such as hatchetfish, often appear silvery because they have mirror-like scales on their body. The scales reflect light when the fish move up into the sunlit areas of the ocean and creates a type of camouflage against the sky above. Hatchetfish and lanternfish also make light in photophores on their belly. When seen from below, this light blends in with the sunlight coming from above, and creates an extra camouflage. In deep waters, some fish are so difficult to see that they have to make their own lights to help their mates to find them!

SEEING IN THE DARK Some deep sea animals use light to find food, while others use it to avoid becoming lunch. Strawberry squid have one small blue eye that scans the dark water below, searching for the flashing lights made by lantern fish and other animals of the deep. A second eye, which is large and yellow, points up looking for prey in the sunlit waters. Atolla jellyfish, meanwhile, flash a dazzling blue light to startle predators that get too close. They hope this will give them just enough time to make a quick getaway!

Megamouth shark **Hatchetfish** **Atolla jellyfish**

I had great fun shining my torch through the submersible's windows, as the HATCHETFISH'S silvery scales reflected the magic beam perfectly. They looked like sheets of glitter as they swam past. Even the red camouflage of an ATOLLA JELLYFISH was useless at hiding its bell-shaped outline and long tentacles from the magic of the torch.

It was exciting to see a rare goblin shark, but I was totally shocked to see a MEGAMOUTH SHARK, its vast body looming in the distance. As it approached it opened it wide jaws and I saw it suck up huge mouthfuls of shrimp. My magic torch has revealed many ocean secrets to me, but this majestic shark has been one of my favourite discoveries so far.

Can you find...
- A megamouth shark?
- A hatchetfish?
- An atolla jellyfish?

Shine your magic torch!

THE HIGH SEAS

Atlantic Ocean

As we voyage north once more, we find ourselves far out to sea with no land in sight; it's an ideal situation for spotting some of the sea's fastest swimmers. At first glance, the open ocean can seem lifeless, apart from birds that soar above the waves, but occasionally a spinner dolphin leaps out of the water and shoals of shimmering fish race past us. There is plenty of action underwater too — that's why Millie is diving in the water. She is going to help me monitor the speeds of the world's fastest shark: the shortfin mako.

→ **RECORD BREAKER** The open ocean is a vast habitat, stretching for thousands of kilometres, with nowhere to hide. The animals that live often rely on speed to chase prey... or escape from danger! I'm using special cameras on board the boat and on my drone to assess the speed of bluefin tuna fish and shortfin mako sharks. According to my equipment, the shark that is now heading towards Millie reached here at a 90 kilometres an hour. The previous top speed was 74 kilometres an hour, so we have just witnessed a record-breaking shark!

Built for speed Even bluefin tunas can swim at 70 kilometres an hour — the speeds achieved by these ocean predators is breath-taking. They manage it because they have tube-shaped bodies that slip easily through water, with powerful, muscle-packed tails.

Tunas, spinner dolphins and makos pursue huge shoals of fish, such as Atlantic mackerel, that also live in these waters. When the fish are under attack, the whole shoal swirls and spins in one large, silvery mass. This confuses the predators, but they rarely go hungry for long.

LONG DISTANCE TRAVELLERS The leatherback turtle is another record-breaker. It is the largest sea turtle and can grow bigger than me! Leatherbacks eat jellyfish, and dive deeper than any other turtle — up to 1,280 metres — to find them. They also go on some of the world's longest journeys, easily travelling more than 1,000 kilometres across the ocean to reach their nesting sites at the coast. In fact, at the Aquarium we have been following the journey of one leatherback turtle that has just swum a staggering 20,000 kilometres across the Pacific Ocean and back again.

Bluefin tuna

Leatherback turtle

Moon jellyfish

I wasn't too sure about cage diving, but I'm so glad I was brave enough to give it a go. Can you imagine what it felt like to have a shark speeding towards you, with its jaws agape? At first I thought it was after me, but I had my magic torch and, using its magic beam, I could see the shark was much more interested in a young BLUEFIN TUNA!

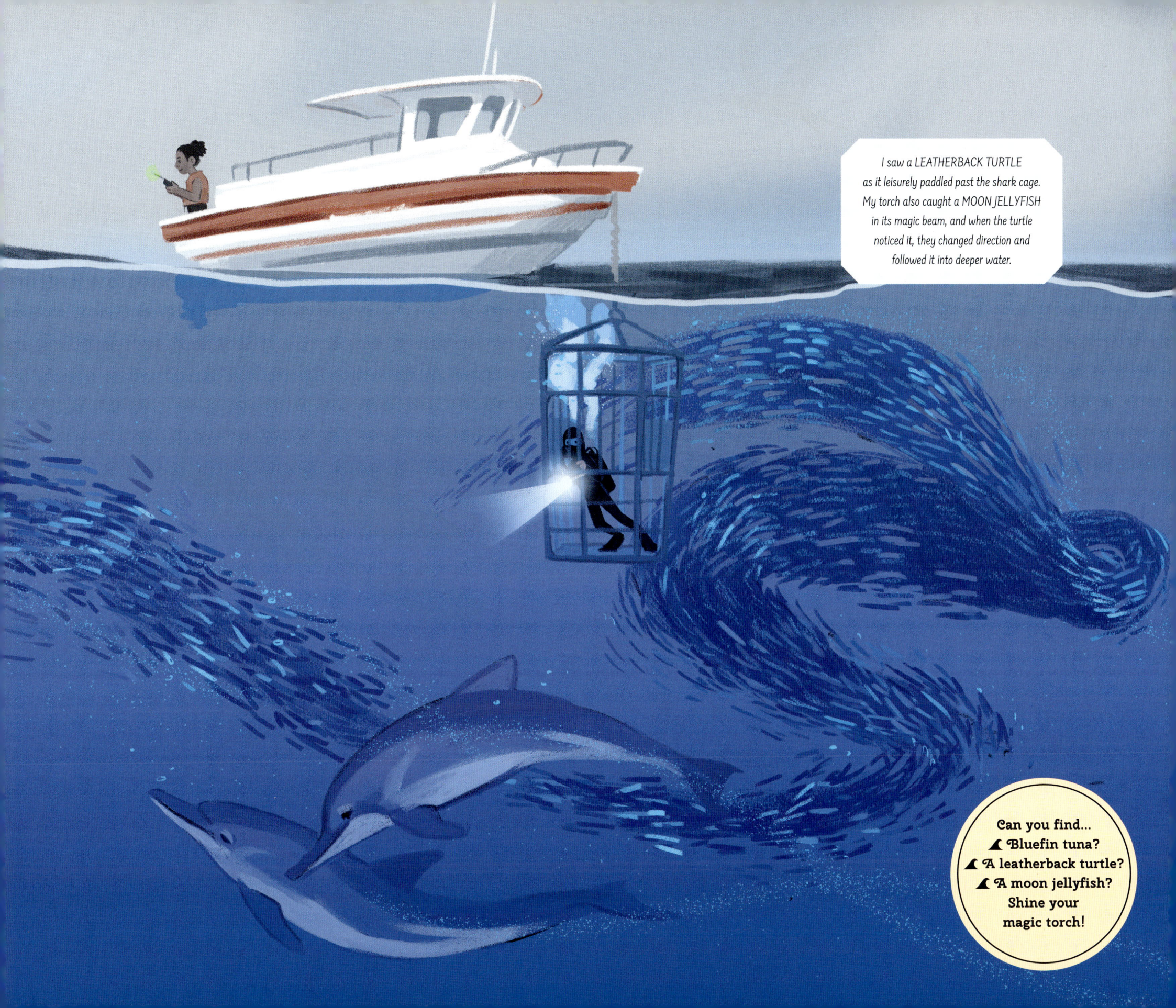

I saw a LEATHERBACK TURTLE as it leisurely paddled past the shark cage. My torch also caught a MOON JELLYFISH in its magic beam, and when the turtle noticed it, they changed direction and followed it into deeper water.

Can you find...
- Bluefin tuna?
- A leatherback turtle?
- A moon jellyfish?

Shine your magic torch!

COASTAL SEABED

Oyster Bay, Atlantic Ocean

We are nearing the end of our adventure, but first we are visiting a unique habitat to search for oysters, stargazers and living fossils. It's a place where salty seawater mixes with the fresh river water which creates a special home for wildlife, but it is under threat. I am here to investigate how the local marine biologists have been working to protect the bay, and I'm on the lookout for the majestic blue crab. At the last count, there were more than 400 million of them, so we should be able to find at least one, even though they are good at hiding!

→ **OYSTERS AND CRABS** Oyster bay is famous for its — you guessed it — oysters! They used to live here in such huge numbers that they created large rocky reefs. The oysters provide food for other animals and they naturally clean the water by filtering the plankton out of it as they feed. The other famous residents of Oyster Bay are blue crabs but, just like the oysters, their numbers have been falling for years. The biologists who work here think the loss of so many oysters and crabs is partly due to pollution from the rivers, and the damage that has been done to the seagrass beds in the bay.

HIDE-AND-SEEK It's a real challenge to find creatures here as thick clumps of seagrass make the perfect hiding place for blue crabs and striped bass. I spotted a large mute swan dipping its long neck into the water to feed on the seagrass, which is bad news — mute swans have moved into this bay and have been stripping the beds. They've caused so much damage to the grass that the fish and crabs have fewer places to hide from predators. The areas without much seagrass may be the best place to look for the northern stargazer fish. It lies on the seabed and covers itself with sand and mud, so it is hidden. When crabs or fish swim past it opens its huge mouth and sucks them in!

> **Living fossil** The horseshoe crab may have the name of a crab, and look like one too, but it is actually more closely related to spiders. This 'living fossil' has survived for at least 445 million years lives in Oyster Bay all year round. It should be easy to spot horseshoe crabs because it is springtime, which is when they leave the seabed and swim towards the shallow shore. On nights when there is a full moon they swarm on to the beach and lay their eggs. Strangely, horseshoe crabs swim upside-down.

Northern stargazer

Blue crab

Horseshoe crab

I was paddling through the seagrass, looking at the striped bass, when a swan tried to peck at me. My torch fell out of my hands and sank to the seabed. As I picked it up, its magic beam shone on the sandy bottom, and I spotted a NORTHERN STARGAZER hiding. So cool! I also caught sight of a HORSESHOE CRAB, making its way to the shore... and it was swimming upside-down. What a strange animal!

Uncle William told me that scientists have released two billion baby oysters into the bay to help restore their numbers which is great. The reef was busy with life and I could see lots of little fish darting in and out of the crevices but my torch found what Uncle William was looking for – a BLUE CRAB. It was crushing a shellfish in its mighty pincers!

Can you find...
◂ A northern stargazer?
◂ A blue crab?
◂ A horseshoe crab?
Shine your magic torch!

ARCTIC SEA ICE

Greenland, Arctic Ocean

What an amazing adventure we have had travelling around the world – just like the amazing Arctic terns we previously met. Millie and I have arrived to Greenland to catch up with the birds we first saw in Antarctica. Since then, the Arctic terns have flown the whole length of the Atlantic Ocean and have arrived here to nest, lay their eggs and raise their chicks. While I was counting the terns I noticed a glorious white-tailed eagle soaring above the ocean. It suddenly swooped low over the water, then dipped down to snatch an Arctic cod out of the sea with its mighty talons!

→ **MIGRATION MYSTERY** Millie and I checked the transmitters on the terns' legs, and some of these birds managed to fly 670 kilometres a day on their return flight. We have worked out that, in one year, an Arctic tern flies 70,000 kilometres and during its lifetime it can fly the equivalent of journeying three times to the Moon and back. What an incredible life these birds have! It is still a mystery to me how they manage to make these epic journeys, but I think they are using the Earth's magnetic field… and perhaps they follow the movement of the sun in the sky? I hope to find out one day.

OCEAN BEARS Polar bears are camouflaged in thick, white fur so they can hide on the sea ice but they are strong swimmers and often dive into the icy cold Arctic water. In winter, mother bears give birth to their cubs in snow dens but, in springtime, the new family emerges into the sunlight. Polar bears hunt fish and seals, but they can attack humans, so Millie and I must keep a safe distance. When a mother polar bear leaves her den she is starving after months of not eating, so she will be on the lookout for hooded seals to eat.

Songs of the Arctic

I have received reports that marine biologists on a boat further out to sea have picked up the sounds of blue whales singing loudly – they are one of the loudest animals on the planet. This is exciting news because blue whales are rarely spotted this far north. They are the biggest animals to have ever lived (that we know of!) so they should be easy to spot. I will keep an eye out for the tell-tale sign of a spout – like other whales, they have to come to the surface to breathe and as they exhale they produce a spout of smelly, steamy water from the blowholes on top of their heads.

Hooded seal

Blue whale

Arctic cod

Straight away my magic torch revealed a HOODED SEAL resting on an ice floe. While I was watching the seal, I caught sight of a fabulous whale spout – it rose above the surface of the water like a fountain, and when I shone my torch at it, a magnificent BLUE WHALE was revealed below. There were even ARCTIC COD swimming nearby. I think they were following the whale as it scooped up mouthfuls of plankton – it's their favourite food too!

Wow! I have visited some amazing ocean habitats and, thanks to my magic torch, I have discovered some mysterious sea creatures. I've enjoyed it all, but the most important thing I've learned is that our oceans are precious places. We must protect them for the future of all of the animals that call them home.

Can you find...
◄ A hooded seal?
◄ A blue whale?
◄ An Arctic cod?
Shine your magic torch!

CAN YOU FIND?

Use your magic torch to go back through the book and find many more mysterious ocean creatures in every scene...

Fiddler crab
In the murky mangrove water, a fiddler crab is almost invisible. At mating time, a male climbs onto the tree roots and waves his big claw about to attract females.

Tundra swan
When a tundra swan takes to the air its wings spread out to an impressive 1.6 metres, sometimes more! These large birds nest in and around the Arctic.

California sea lion
Unlike other sea lions, playful California sea lions do not have lionlike manes. Sea lions are superb swimmers, chasing shoals of fish at great speed.

Vent octopus

This deep-sea octopus is incredibly pale. It has little need for colour or camouflage in a world where neither predator nor prey is likely to see them.

Arctic tern

Almost invisible against the blue-grey sky, an Arctic tern continues its incredible annual migration as it flies to enjoy a year of endless summers.

Leopard shark

This shark is camouflaged in the dappled shadows of the seabed. It leaves the safety of its hiding place to hunt in the sunlit shallows.

Lined seahorse

Rings of bony plates cover this lined seahorse's body. These creatures are poor swimmers that rely on their camouflage ability to hide from predators.

Giant clam
This giant clam is a mighty beast that can grow more than a metre wide. It is one of many endangered coral creatures, so spotting one of these is a rare treat!

Tasselled wobbegong
A master of disguise, this flat-bodied shark has been compared to a patterned rug on the seabed. Its tassels blur its outline, making it almost impossible to spot.

Crocodile icefish
Most fish would find the waters of the Southern Ocean too cold, but icefish prefer water that is almost cold enough to freeze. They reach 50 centimetres in length.

Red jellyfish
Known as Benthocodon, this red jellyfish is just 3 centimetres long. It uses stingers on its arms to kill even smaller prey.

Hagfish
Hagfish have survived for 500 million years. They have four hearts, are covered in thick slime and can tie themselves up in knots!

Crinoid
Crinoids are related to starfish. They are attached to the seabed and pull food into their mouths using long, feathery arms.

Flying fish
Flying fish leap out of the water to escape the jaws of hungry predators. They use their large fins to glide more than 50 metres at a time.

Antarctic midge
The largest land animal in the Antarctic is an insect no bigger than a grain of rice. No one knows how these little midges can cope with the icy-cold climate.

Atlantic puffin
With their comical faces and colourful feathers, these birds are often called 'parrots of the sea'. Puffins nest underground in burrows.

Eleven-armed sea star
Despite its name, this starfish can actually have up to fourteen arms, and grows to an impressive 40 centimetres wide. Eleven-armed sea stars eat worms and crabs.

MAGIC CAT PUBLISHING

Published in 2023 by Magic Cat Publishing, an imprint of Lucky Cat
Publishing Ltd, Unit 2 Empress Works, 24 Grove Passage, London E2 9FQ, UK

Text, illustrations and layout © Ronshin Group 2022

No part of this publication may be reproduced, stored in a retrieval system, or transmitted,
in any form, or by any means, electrical, mechanical, photocopying, recording or otherwise
without the prior written permission of the publisher or a licence permitting restricted copying.

A catalogue record for this book is available from the British Library.

ISBN 978-1-913520-99-1

The illustrations were created in gouache and watercolour
Set in Bourton, Cherry Swash, Farsan, Josefin Sans and Penny Serenade

Created by Magic Cat Publishing, an imprint of Lucky Cat Publishing Ltd,
Unit 2 Empress Works, 24 Grove Passage, London E2 9FQ, UK

Written by Camilla de la Bedoyere
Illustrated by Alexandria Neonakis
Cover design by Ella Tomkins
Designed by Nicola Price and Joe Hales
Edited by Helen Brown
Consultancy by Professor Dorrik Stow

Manufactured in China, LEO0723

9 8 7 6 5 4 3 2 1

MIX
Paper | Supporting
responsible forestry
FSC® C020056